Quiet I
Style

Elegant fashion for Ladies after 50

by Lady Henrietta Jones-Hunter

&

Sarah Jones

Creating a wardrobe marked by elegance,
poise, timeless beauty,
& sustainability

The Privilege of Age

Where did I first hear that? 'Aging is a privilege, not everyone gets to do it.' It is true that as the years accumulate so does wisdom and elegance. When did you last see an elegant teenager? There is nothing more powerful than discovering our own unique beauty and allowing our very best qualities to blossom.
Even Menopause is a transition that we can embrace, and prepare for—with some beautiful and simple adjustments in our wardrobe.

Inside this little guide, you will find ways to evolve into the most elegant version of yourself. Shopping shortcuts, quiet luxury cheat sheets, 'old-money' style secrets, little-known tailoring tips, beautifully simple, but effective, beauty routines; the whole package.

This little booklet is part of a series of fun, easy to read guides packed with a wealth of information.

Log out, stretch out, make yourself comfortable, soaking in the quiet luxury of having un enjoyable read!

Nothing more powerful than a woman of a 'certain age' embracing her own unique beauty.

contents

Welcome the Goddess of Quiet Luxury

Ladies, welcome to the club! You have arrived. Whether you are approaching your fifties or have already embraced this decade and beyond—congratulations. You are now a woman of substance, wisdom, and allure. A force to be reckoned with. Time to reveal our inner goddess.

This is no time to shrink back or fade into the background. Now it's time to own our presence, our style, and our undeniable elegance. Think of it as evolution rather than aging—a grand opportunity to create a lifestyle marked by grace, poise, and an appreciation for timeless beauty.

There is something reassuring about the 'grande dame,' the classic 'old money' style. An implication of wisdom, affluence, and success that we can now enjoy.

Our wardrobe is not just about clothes—it's also about the essence we bring into the world. What kind of energy do we exude? What presence do you wish to command? Dressing well is an art, a ritual, a celebration of the evolving self. Of course, you could still wear hot pants if you truly wanted to—but why on earth would you? Let the younger generation endure discomfort while you luxuriate in refinement, confidence, and ease. You are like a perfectly aged Château Margaux—complex, exquisite, and only the more desirable as time goes by.

For far too long, women have been bombarded with 'anti-aging' propaganda, as if growing older was somehow your fault. Society has treated mature women as though allowing themselves to look their age is a failure, while simultaneously ridiculing those who seek to maintain a youthful appearance. The rules are contradictory. The game is rigged.

But you, my dear lady, are beyond all that. You are stepping into your prime. This is the era of quiet luxury, of sartorial excellence, of dressing with purpose and pleasure. Now is the time to relish your wardrobe, to revel in the rituals of getting dressed, to treasure high-quality pieces that have stood the test of time and to carefully select new acquisitions with discernment.

If you have the means to invest in timeless luxury, wonderful! If not, your wisdom will guide you to the smartest, most elegant choices. Because you know who you are and what you love. What if you're still discovering? This guide will be your trusted companion, leading you toward a wardrobe of finesse, style and effortless sophistication.

You have arrived. Let's celebrate it.

Inside the Quiet Luxury Wardrobe

It's nice to start by taking a little peak into the quiet luxury wardrobe of this divine woman...

Imagine this beautifully crafted dressing area—perhaps not exactly a grand walk-in closet, but it is a serene, well-ordered space with solid wooden shelves, softly glowing lamps, and a full length mirror. Clothes are arranged with care, every single piece carefully chosen by the elegant owner of this calming space.

The ideal quiet luxury wardrobe isn't about having lots of clothes; it's about *curation*. A space that reflects a life well-lived, filled with exquisite, wearable pieces that bring ease, confidence, and quiet refinement. (There is also another space somewhere in this house that contains the memorabilia, and all the clothes that are no longer used. They are already in boxes and they may or may not go to a charity store in six months time.)

Right here though, there is a row of freshly ironed linen and cotton shirts in white, cream and soft blues. A stack of cotton t-shirts in neutrals and classic tones hangs neatly beside a selection of well-cut trousers—each pressed to perfection, ready to be worn at a moment's notice. Nearby, the softest cashmere sweaters, loosely folded and layered with acid-free tissue, offer both luxury and practicality. A couple of pure silk blouses—one with delicate pearl buttons—provide effortless polish for any occasion. Next there are a couple of tailored jackets—perhaps one is vintage Chanel? Perhaps not. The logo isn't important; the craftsmanship speaks for itself.

Dark-wash denim shares space with three or four dresses in cotton, linen and silk. They have pride of place and are ready to go at a moments notice, ready with their coordinated belt and accessories thoughtfully positioned on the same hanger.

Beautifully organised lingerie and sleepwear—though, naturally, a few mismatched socks still find their way into the drawers. This quiet luxury woman stuffs her single socks with dried lavender bought from holidays in Provence. Subsequently she uses them as wardrobe fresheners and moth deterrents.

Out-of-season pieces are tucked at the back, while outerwear—an impeccably tailored wool coat, a classic trench—hang in a separate section, ready for cooler days. If she lives in a cold climate there is usually a selection of well tailored coats and classic puffer jackets collected over the years.

Eveningwear, though not excessive, is thoughtfully stored in protective garment bags. There's a perfect black dress for a formal event, an elegant gown for holiday gatherings, and a refined cocktail dress that never fails to impress.

A dedicated space for leisurewear includes her yoga sets, soft loungewear, and classic tennis whites—because style should never be sacrificed, even when at ease. The drawers may not always be as impeccably arranged as the labels suggest, but they hold what is needed: quality, timeless pieces that fit seamlessly into an elegant life.

In front of a full-length triptych mirror stands a small, upholstered chair—the perfect place to sit while selecting accessories. A carefully edited collection of silk scarves, three or four go-to handbags, and a few exquisite pieces of jewellery rest in a velvet-lined tray. No excess, no clutter—just thoughtful refinement.

Thank the gods this wardrobe is not for Instagram; it is for living. This quiet luxury woman spends more time enjoying her clothes than shopping for them.

A collection of suitable outfits for every occasion, especially for the simplest of days, where 'nothing much 'happens'. For those are the days of which life is made.

The actual clothes may vary, depending on lifestyle, location, and personal taste. Yet, the principles remain the same: high quality, comfort, and sophistication that grows more powerful with age.

Menopause: Dressing for Comfort, Elegance & Confidence

Beautiful clothes, breathable fabrics, layering strategies, and looking polished while staying cool.

Sadly, many women at this stage of life feel overlooked and gradually slip into wearing shapeless tracksuits and athleisure in indeterminate colours. To make matters worse, much of this unflattering athleisure is made from synthetic fabrics—nylon, polyester, and spandex—that trap heat, prevent the skin from breathing, and contribute to discomfort. Worse still, these materials are often treated with chemicals such as phthalates and BPA, both of which have been linked to endocrine disruption. During menopause, when hormones are already fluctuating, exposure to these chemicals can further imbalance the system, thus exacerbating symptoms like hot flushes, fatigue, and skin irritation. But let's be clear—this stage of life is not about fading into the background in drab, lifeless fabrics. Embrace elegant, breathable clothing that enhances your natural beauty and confidence. Swap synthetic, clingy fabrics for the quiet luxury of pure linen, soft cashmere, and flowing silk. Try on some wide-leg trousers or an easy midi skirt that provide elegance without clinging, and can pair beautifully with airy tops. You can always use a belt if you think it needs some extra definition.

Menopause is a time of change and transition. While medical support is available to ease this shift, true comfort often comes from simple yet powerful self-care tools: eating healthy, freshly-made food, short yoga routines, regular exercise, and evolving our wardrobes to beautifully serve our changing lifestyle.

If you are not already a convert, this is the time to focus on natural breathable fabrics. Embrace clothing that works with you, not against you. Natural breathable fabrics, clever layering, and a few well-chosen silhouettes can help you stay cool and polished. Now *that's* quiet luxury at its finest.

When shopping for new clothes, start with the breathable base layers—a soft silk camisole under a linen button-down or a flowing cotton tunic that moves with your body. Linen or pure cotton shirt dresses or a refined A-line cut. The ultimate 'throw-on-and-go' solution. You look put-together with minimal effort.

In the following pages we will look into some options for refreshing the closet and new wardrobe additions.

New underwear

Buying new underwear is the apotheosis of quiet luxury at any stage in life but especially around menopause time! Natural fabrics like cotton, silk, or bamboo will keep you cool and comfortable. Ditch anything too tight or synthetic, as it can trap heat and make hot flushes worse. A well-fitted bra in a smooth, supportive shape (preferably with no underwire digging in) can transform how your clothes sit on your body.

Old bras that are the wrong size and dig into your skin have absolutely no place in your revamped underwear drawer. Quality, comfortable bras are a life changing experience. They will quite literally form the foundation of your chic ensemble. Pure silk soft bras are a luxury and sateen cotton ones are lovely for everyday. Special t-shirt bras will ensure a smooth seamless look.

The very best lingerie comes from France and Italy, of course. But don't be tempted to start ordering online just yet. The first step in curating an elegant lingerie drawer is booking an appointment for a bra fitting. Ideally at a specialist boutique. A well-fitted bra is transformative—not just in how your clothes sit but in how you carry yourself and even how you breath. Give yourself a gift and retire the stretched-out bras, synthetic lace, and uncomfortable frills. Quiet luxury begins with quality, in the smallest of details.

Spandex and those so called 'shapers,' are really uncomfortable at the best of times. During menopause they may well be considered as instruments of torture, so just say no.

Indulge in beauty & quality

Let us indulge a little! Look for washable, **silk French knickers, beautiful cotton or linen nightdresses**, **soft pure cotton pyjamas**, and at least one **elegant dressing gown**. Allow yourself to feel beautiful and comfortable at all times. Effortless at-home luxury.

Keep a small collection of high-quality freshly laundered undergarments on hand—soft bralettes, lightweight camisoles, and airy French knickers. The luxury of slipping into fresh lingerie throughout the day or whenever you feel uncomfortably overheated is an understated yet powerful form of self-care, helping to maintain a feeling of elegance, ease, and well-being.

Caring for Sensitive skin during menopause: fabrics & laundry considerations

During menopause as skin becomes thinner, drier, and more reactive, even the most luxurious fabrics can cause irritation if they are washed in harsh detergents or treated with chemicals. A simple switch can make all the difference—start using **hypoallergenic, fragrance-free washing powders** formulated for sensitive skin (detergents designed for baby skin often work better). Stop using heavily scented fabric softeners, as these can leave residue on your clothes that may cause itching or discomfort. Instead, opt for **mild, eco-friendly detergents** and use less of the actual product. Definitely no fabreeze or artificial odour removers.

It may be best to wash new clothes before wearing them and keeping old clothes for as long as possible. Good quality items get softer and more comfortable with wash and wear.

Dry Cleaning Caution

Many dry-cleaning chemicals can be harsh on sensitive skin, so be mindful of how often you send items for treatment. If possible, choose easy machine washable or hand-washable versions of garments that touch your skin directly—such as silk camisoles, blouses, or even tailored trousers lined with natural fibres.

Now more than ever, it's worth seeking out clothing made from undyed, chemical-free, and OEKO-TEX®-certified fabrics to ensure that what sits against your skin is as pure and non-irritating as possible.

The Luxury of Freshness

Slipping into freshly laundered undergarments can feel very calming and provide instant comfort and renewal. For an added touch of quiet luxury, store your delicates with lightly scented linen sachets or place a few drops of pure essential oils, such as lavender or chamomile, on a cloth inside your wardrobe—ensuring they never come into direct contact with the fabric, or your skin. This subtle scent infusion can enhance relaxation, turning each change of clothing into a soothing act of self-care.

Easy dress styles to remain comfortable and chic Quiet Luxury style

What could be simpler than wearing a comfortable dress and your favourite trainers or loafers? Ditch the athleisure wear and replace with:

Shirt Dresses:Timeless and elegant, with or without the addition of a belt. Cool & comfortable.
Wrap Dresses: Universally flattering and easy to tailor for a precise fit. Look for breathable fabrics, but with elegant drape.
Tailored Sheath Dresses: A custom-fit sheath dress skims the body without clinging.
Flowy Silk (or Linen) dress: Loose-fitting sleeveless or with billowy sleeves to allow the skin to breathe!

Less choice actually means more elegance! Remember you really don't need ALL of those styles of dresses. You can just pick one and perfect it. Different body types will suit one or two dress styles, so experiment and edit. Then edit again! Look at your lifestyle and evaluate realistically your personal needs highlighting what you love most about yourself.

One really comfortable dress in natural fabric is worth more to you than a dozen fast fashion, ill fitting polyester dresses. Thats the moto!

Dresses are very adaptable to suit various occasions. Accessorise them and you can change the mood of the outfit, using different belts, shoes, hairstyles, jewellery, bags and even glasses. Lets take an example of a **plain blue chambray dress** accessorised in different ways:

Look 1: Polished Daytime Elegance

Hairstyle: A smooth low bun or a neat ponytail.
Earrings: Small pearl studs.
Accessories: A slim leather belt, classic loafers structured tote bag.
Vibe: Sophisticated, effortless, perfect for a café meeting, casual lunch, or gallery visit.

Look 2: Relaxed Weekend Chic

Hairstyle: Loose waves or a soft, messy braid.
Earrings: Colourful enamel clip ons, or hoops
Accessories: A woven belt espadrilles, a neat little crossbody bag.

Hot Tip: If you wear sleeveless dresses you can always try using a linen shirt on top, unbuttoned like a cardigan, but so cool! If you prefer sleeves, opt for cotton or linen and choose very **loose, billowy sleeves** to avoid unsightly sweat patches.

A Wardrobe of Distinction

Curating a collection of elegant, timeless pieces that reflect your life experience and personal style.

The quiet luxury wardrobe that is just absolutely perfect for you, is broadly a matter of lifestyle. (*Do you still work full time, are you retired, a keen gardener, an equestrian or an amateur painter?*) It is also location dependent (*do you live somewhere cold, does it rain a lot or is it mostly sweltering heat?*) and to some extent, budget dependant. (*No, don't answer that yet!*) There are however some universal principles to follow.

Quality over quantity

Now is the time to curate a wardrobe that serves you, not the other way around. Gone are the days of an overstuffed closet filled with impulse buys and crazy trends. This is the essence of quiet luxury—not a loud display of wealth but full of the quiet assurance of quality and refined taste.

The foundation? **Quality over quantity.** A single, exquisitely tailored black dress that fits like a dream is worth more to you than ten ill-fitting ones. A grey cashmere coat that drapes just so, will carry you through most occasions, while a well-cut pair of navy trousers will always be a style essential

Fewer, better pieces made from luxurious natural fabrics like organic cotton, quality cashmere, silk, linen, and fine wool.

Flattering fit & tailoring

Tailoring is everything. A perfect fit makes an outfit, no matter the price tag. The secret to looking polished isn't a designer label—it's precision. A cinched waist where needed, a hemline that flatters, a sleeve that grazes the wrist at just the right spot. These details separate the stylish from those who are merely dressed.

Prioritise impeccable fit. Well-tailored clothing enhances confidence and ensures elegance at any age. It may be useful to work with an experienced tailor to refine silhouettes to perfection. Or sewing lessons for simple alterations, like hemming or button replacement.

Timeless, versatile style

Reaching for a classic silk blouse, still as indulgent as the day you bought it, slipping on those gorgeous, Italian leather loafers that have moulded perfectly to your step, wrapping yourself in a generous Scottish cashmere scarf that whispers elegance rather than shouting for attention.

Choosing classic, enduring designs means you no longer need to follow trends, dear ladies. (*Ok maybe just a slight nod but only to the trends that you actually love!*) A neutral palette, think charcoal grey, chocolate brown, bottle green, wine red, cream or pure white. Adding some of your favourite colours as little accents ensures effortless coordination and refinement in every single outfit. Why we could get dressed in the dark! (But we won't. We always use a full length mirror to help.)

Of course, timeless doesn't mean dated, we will go over this later. We have tips and tricks to wear classic clothes in ways that feel fresh and contemporary

Effortless & refined

The key to quiet luxury is looking polished without appearing overdone. Less is more, every detail matters.

How you wear your jewellery, how you style your hair, and choosing the right accessories and not too many of them! By the time we get to 50, we should have at least some idea of what we like and what actually suits our life. For example, we may by now have worked out that high heels are absolutely killing us and a lovely pair of trainers helps with posture. That is effortless elegance for you.

Subtle accessorising, high-quality basics, and a well-maintained wardrobe help create that quiet luxury aura of sophistication and ease. More importantly, they actually do make life a lot easier. Easy relaxed living!

Quality Control: What to Keep in the Quiet Luxury Wardrobe

By the time you reach 50, you've likely amassed a wardrobe filled with memories—pieces from past careers, impulse buys, sentimental treasures, and 'just in case' outfits that never quite made it into the world.

Style evolves alongside experiences, and now is the perfect time to refine it. This isn't about starting over; it's about evolving to curate a wardrobe that truly serves you—one that reflects who you are today, not who you used to be or who you might be one day.

I am afraid there is no avoiding it: start with a clear-out, but don't be too hasty. Gather some sturdy boxes and begin sorting. Label them: **Keep, Store, Donate, Mend, and Maybe.** Store away anything with sentimental value or seasonal wear. Mend what can be restored to its former glory. Older clothes are usually better quality so hang on to as much as you can. Donate pieces that no longer align with your style but could bring joy to someone else. And for the 'maybes'—give yourself time. Fashion should be like an effortless luxury, not an overwhelming source of stress!

With only your very best pieces remaining in your wardrobe, getting dressed each day becomes a quiet luxury in itself.

Quality checklist

Quiet Luxury fashion is all about quality with a sense of timelessness. Younger women usually have more trouble recognising quality, simply because they've never actually had the good fortune to experience it.

Anything you decide to keep in your new quiet luxury wardrobe should pass the quality test with flying colours. Anything you decide to buy new should most definitely be a better option, than what is already in your closet.

In any case refer to the quality checklist and of course feel free to add you own very specific demands. In the quality checklist we look for:

1. Quality Fabric
2. Good Cut
3. Refined Finish.

Keeping everything in its place, and a place for everything, is a key luxury.

'Noble' Fabrics: The essential quality for luxury

Wool, cashmere, alpaca, linen, hemp, silk, and cotton—these natural fibres are often referred to as 'noble' fabrics. They are the foundation of true quiet luxury. They also age beautifully, growing softer and more characterful over time. Wearing natural materials isn't just about aesthetics; it's about comfort, breathability, and the way fabric interacts with the body.

This becomes especially important during menopause, a stage where many women experience heightened sensitivity to synthetic fibres. Hot flashes, fluctuating body temperature, and changes in skin tolerance can make polyester, acrylic, and other artificial fabrics feel stifling, scratchy, or even irritating. Natural fibres, on the other hand, allow the skin to breathe and regulate body temperature—keeping you cool when you're warm and providing essential warmth when you need it.

There is also a quiet, tactile pleasure in wearing high-quality, organic materials. The softness of cashmere against the skin, the crispness of freshly pressed linen, the fluidity of silk—they offer a sensory experience that synthetic fabrics simply cannot compete with. Investing in these noble textiles is not just a choice of style but one of self-care, embracing luxury that works in harmony with your body as it evolves.

Good cut matters more than ever

The right 'cut' enhances posture, flatters the figure, and makes clothes feel as good as they look. If we still have older clothes in our wardrobe, some of which may be of superb quality, (pre 1990s pieces so often are). If at all possible consider taking them to a tailor for some thoughtful alterations to get the fit just so.

As an example of an item of clothing with a flattering good 'cut', we take the bias-cut skirt. It requires more fabric than its mass-produced counterparts but drapes fluidly over the body, moving with effortless grace. A traditional Chanel jacket—iconic for a reason—is constructed from 20 to 25 separate pieces of material, each shaped and stitched to flatter the body. If you have any such pieces that no longer fit s—definitely worth looking for a good tailor.

As our bodies change, investing in tailoring ensures our elegance evolves with us at any age.

Quiet luxury finesse & construction

Silk linings, French seams, blind hems, and perfectly matched patterns—these details were once standard in well-made garments but are now increasingly rare. I can't even remember the last time I came across a new item of clothing with a blind hem, even in relatively expensive clothes. Yet, these seemingly small touches make all the difference in how well a piece drapes, moves, and lasts over time.

For the quiet luxury woman, investing in impeccable construction is worth every penny. 'Construction' is different from 'fit' and cut. Something may be perfect construction, but poor fit on our body. (*This can usually be corrected, with tailoring.*) Ideally you want both good fit and quality construction.

These details not only elevate the look of an outfit but also enhance comfort, making garments feel more luxurious to wear. A silk-lined blazer glides effortlessly over the skin, eliminating the static of synthetic linings. French seams prevent raw edges from fraying, ensuring longevity. A properly finished hem remains invisible yet provides the perfect weight for fabric to fall beautifully.

While these elements may not be immediately noticeable to the untrained eye, they make all the difference. When curating your wardrobe, seek out these refined details—or consider having them added to elevate the pieces you already love.

Classic fashion but not frumpy fashion

There's a fine line between classic and frumpy—a line the stylish woman must never cross. A quiet luxury wardrobe embraces classic elements, but always with a refined, modern edge. Yes to plain cashmere sweaters in solid colours, beautifully tailored jackets, simple dresses and impeccably cut shirts. No to exaggerated details, like oversized lapels or fussy silhouettes. Anything too baggy or skin-tight is a no.

You know those old photos where you're wearing the height of fashion at the time, and now you can't help but laugh at how ridiculous it looks? That's the effect of trends taken too far. True classics, on the other hand, never make you wince in horror.

The irony is that the best, most timeless clothes often have the most intricate construction yet appear deceptively simple. A perfectly tailored blazer is understated, but its structure, fabric, and cut make all the difference. The same goes for a silk slip dress or a beautifully draped coat. Classic style is wearing your pieces and accessorising them to be more you.

Examples of details that date an item of clothing

Exaggerated Large Lapels: Often seen in suits and jackets from the 1970s, these can make an item look outdated.
Oversized Shoulder Pads: Popular in the 1980s, especially in women's blazers and dresses, these can make garments look vintage rather than timeless.
Ultra Low-Rise Jeans: A hallmark of early 2000s fashion, these can make pants look dated (compared to the current preference for high-rise styles, ultra high rise is likely to be also a passing trend)
Embellished Denim: Rhinestones, embroidery, and heavy embellishments on jeans were popular in the early 2000s but are now considered passé. The only exception would be with something exceptionally well made, handmade embroidery, that sort of thing. Quality never goes out of style.
Peplum Tops: While they had a resurgence in the 2010s, peplum tops and dresses can quickly look outdated as trends move on.
Bell-Bottoms and Flared Pants: Although they come back into style periodically, they are very much associated with the 1970s.
Logomania: Over-the-top branding, which was especially popular in the 1990s and early 2000s. More understated branding is currently in vogue, even better no branding at all.

Cargo Pants: Particularly those from the late 1990s and early 2000s, with multiple pockets and a baggy fit, can look *quelle horreur* !
Too many zips/fastenings.
Too short skirts or dresses.
Body con dresses (very 1990's.)
Stone-washed denim.

Examples of details that give an item of clothing timeless appeal

Classic Patterns: Patterns like houndstooth, pinstripes, and checks have a long history in fashion and continue to be seen as stylish and elegant, making garments featuring these patterns timeless.
Neutral Colours: Classic pieces often come in neutral colours like black, white, navy, beige, bottle green, burgundy and most shades of gray. Versatile, easy to mix and match.
Quality Fabric: Classic pieces are often made from high-quality materials like cashmere, alpaca, wool, silk, and high-grade cotton. These fabrics not only wear well over time but also have a luxurious look and feel. Quality is never out of fashion.
Tailored Fit: Clothing with a well-tailored fit, such as a custom fit blazer or a tailored pair of trousers, tends to look polished and sophisticated, regardless of changing fashion trends.

Subtle and Refined Accents: Details like understated custom dyed buttons, delicate stitching, and simple pockets contribute to the timeless appeal of a garment. Accents to add interest without overwhelming.
Simple Silhouettes: Clean, uncomplicated lines and silhouettes ensure that clothing remains elegant and stylish. The old cliche a little black dress, a crisp white shirt, or a trench coat.
Minimalistic Details: It's hard to stress this enough: classic clothing usually features minimalistic design elements. Avoidance of excessive embellishments, logos and patterns ensures that the piece has longevity and utility. They will 'blend' more seamlessly with the odd 'statement' piece.

Classic colour is timeless but never dull

As we refine our style over 50, the power of classic colours becomes even more apparent. Perhaps hair and skin colour has changed and is time to adjust a wardrobe palette that enhances your natural beauty and complements your lifestyle.

Neutrals like navy, camel, ivory, taupe, and deep charcoal are the backbone of a sophisticated wardrobe. These shades exude quiet confidence and never look outdated. Black, while a staple for many, can sometimes feel harsh against mature skin—but if you are the sort of diva that likes to wear bold lipstick, it can still work well.

In any case, do consider softer alternatives like deep espresso brown or midnight blue. They can be far more flattering. Try them out to choose tones that bring out warmth and luminosity rather than washing you out.

That's not to say colour is off-limits—far from it! Colour brings you joy! A well-placed shade of emerald, a rich burgundy, or rose can add interest without looking garish. Jewel tones often work beautifully, lending an air of refinement without feeling overwhelming. Avoid overly bright, synthetic-looking hues, like neons, which can also be difficult to coordinate. Instead lean into elegant, slightly toned down versions of your personal favourite colour.

Think of your wardrobe as a designers collection, more or less all pieces should work together in terms of colour, cut and style. If need be, separate them into seasonal colour sets: one for Autumn /Winter and another for Spring/Summer.

Just like with classic silhouettes, classic colours stand the test of time. A beautifully cut coat in a neutral hue will always look chic, while a silk blouse in a flattering shade of blue or soft blush will never feel out of place. The goal is to build a wardrobe where every piece works in harmony, creating effortless, polished outfits that feel as good as they look.

Reference sheets to pass the quality test

Assessing the quality of clothing, is a typical Quiet Luxury shopping habit. We know better than to rely on logos and labels. The lining, seams, and stitching are key indicators. Not, by any means, the only indicators—but a very good place to start.

1. Lining

Fabric Quality: High-quality garments often use natural fibres like silk, cotton, or viscose for linings. These materials are breathable and comfortable.
Construction: The lining should be smoothly attached, without puckering or pulling, and should match the contours of the garment perfectly.
Coverage: In well-made garments, the lining often extends fully throughout the piece (e.g., in jackets and skirts), rather than being partial or absent.

2. Seams

Consistency: Seams should be even and straight, without puckers or crooked lines. Consistent seam allowances (the fabric between the seam and the edge) are also a sign of quality.
Reinforcement: High-stress areas (like the crotch, underarms, and pockets) should have reinforced stitching or extra fabric (e.g., bar tacks or double stitching) to prevent tearing.

Finishing: Look for well-finished seams, such as French seams, flat-felled seams, or bound seams. These methods encase raw edges, preventing fraying and extending the garment's life.

3. Stitching
Stitch Length and Density: High-quality garments have smaller, tighter stitches (e.g., 8-12 stitches per inch). This ensures durability and a neat appearance.
Backstitching: At the beginning and end of a seam, backstitching should be used to secure the threads. This prevents the seam from unraveling.
Thread Quality: The thread should be strong and chosen to match the garment's colour. Poor-quality thread can deteriorate after just a few washes.

Additional Considerations

Pattern Matching: In high-quality garments, patterns (like stripes or plaids) should align at seams and edges. This shows attention to detail and skill.
Hems: Hems should be even and securely stitched, often with a blind hem stitch to keep them invisible from the outside. An allowance to shorten or lengthen, used is an indicator of quality and adaptability.
Buttonholes and Zippers: Buttonholes should be neatly finished without loose threads. Zippers should glide smoothly and be securely attached, ideally with a covering flap for a discreet, polished look.

Examine these details, to better judge the quality of a garment to make informed purchasing decisions.

Wardrobe Refresh: Re-Styling Clothes You Already Own

So, you have a beautifully cut, 20-year-old tweed skirt suit with an exquisite fit? Lucky you!
A well-made piece like this is a treasure—timeless in quality but easily refreshed for the present day.

Let's take the example of the 20-year-old tweed skirt suit: The secret to keeping it modern? Never wear the full set together (unless you're intentionally channeling 'grandmama chic')—and if you are, please do go all in by adding pearls and a polished ladylike handbag!

Give that old jacket new life by pairing it with a fresh white t-shirt and your favourite dark-wash jeans. The mix of structured tweed and relaxed denim creates that effortless, refined contrast that defines quiet luxury.

As for the tweed skirt? Style it with a fitted Henley top and a (gently) distressed denim jacket for a touch of nonchalant elegance. Add your favourite earrings—gold hoops or sparkly studs—finish with a neat little bag.

Quiet luxury is about knowing how to reinvent what you already own. Favourite old jeans and other high quality pieces can be adjusted and reimagined. You don't have to start your wardrobe from zero, a good tailor who can advise you is your best styling friend.

Tailoring & fit knowhow: the Secret weapon for Quiet Luxury Ladies over 50

Off-the-rack clothing rarely offers a perfect fit for anyone. Especially so for mature figures where subtle adjustments will make all the difference. Skilled tailoring elevates even simple garments, ensuring comfort, elegance, and a polished silhouette.

For a quiet luxury wardrobe, clothes should skim the body, offering structure without restriction. A well-tailored jacket, for example, allows for ease of movement in the shoulders, flatters your natural lines, and regulates body temperature with precision. Poor tailoring, on the other hand, feels awkward, stiff, or unflattering.

Not every item of your old clothing is going to be worthy of alterations (which are usually time consuming and expensive). Still the most sophisticated wardrobes often include bespoke or couture pieces—whether inherited, commissioned, or carefully sourced over time. If you already own high quality clothes altering and customising them is akin to couture. Thoughtful tailoring, well-chosen details, and strategic alterations can rejuvenate these older pieces into a wardrobe of timeless sophistication.

Soft Hourglass
(Defined waist, but with a softer midsection)

Key Tailoring Alterations:

- Light waist shaping in jackets without excessive cinching—side seams can be subtly taken in for definition.
- Raise the waistline on dresses or tops slightly to avoid cutting into the midsection.
- Let out darts or princess seams slightly to prevent fabric pulling at the bust.
- Adjust trouser or skirt linings to ensure a smooth drape, avoiding excess cling.

Styling Recommendations

- Wrap-style or belted coats create definition. Adding one of your own belts can alter the whole look.
- Dresses with subtle ruching or draping across the torso flatter the waist.
- Mid-rise trousers with a tailored leg elongate the figure—avoid those high-rises that emphasise the midsection.
- A structured, softly tailored blazer with a longer hemline balances proportions.

Column/Rectangle
(Straight up and down, minimal waist definition)

Key Tailoring Alterations:

- Add subtle waist darts or a gentle taper in jackets to create the illusion of shape.
- Hem blazers at mid-hip rather than lower, to add structure without overwhelming the frame.
- Shorten sleeves slightly to show the wrist for a refined, deliberate fit.
- Adjust trouser hems to ensure a sleek break at the shoe—cropped lengths work well, but overly long trousers can make the frame look boxy.

Styling Recommendations:

- Double-breasted blazers add structure and create a sense of definition.
- A puffer jacket or a gilet under your more formal tailored coat keeps you warm and toasty.
- A-line skirts or trousers with a subtle flare balance the silhouette beautifully.
- Monochrome or tonal dressing with slight tonal variations elongates the figure while maintaining an understated elegance.

Pear Shape
(Slimmer on top, fuller hips and thighs)

Key Tailoring Alterations:

- Take in the waist of blazers for a closer fit while ensuring room in the hip area—avoid stiff, boxy cuts.
- Adding small shoulder pads in structured jackets balance proportions.
- Ensure trousers or skirts skim the hips without pulling, consider letting out seams slightly if needed.
- Adjust hemlines on coats or skirts to hit just below the knee or at the most flattering point (usually the slimmest point of the leg.)

Styling Recommendations:

- Single-breasted coats with a tailored waist create a flattering line without bulk.
- Straight-leg or wide-leg trousers balance the lower half—avoid skinny cuts that emphasise proportions.
- Darker tones on the bottom half with lighter or structured tops draw attention upwards.
- A classic, minimal leather belt (add one of your own belts for a personalised touch) over a soft, wool coat helps define the waist without cutting into the frame.

Tailoring for your high quality Dresses & Skirts.

Dresses and skirts form the foundation of a refined, quiet luxury wardrobe, but their fit must be perfect to achieve a polished look.

Key Tailoring Adjustments for Dresses:.

- **Waist & Bust Adjustments:** Many dresses can benefit from slight alterations at the waist or bust. A competent tailor can add darts or take in side seams for a more flattering shape.
- **Shoulder Adjustments:** Droopy shoulders can make a dress look ill-fitting. Adjusting shoulder seams or adding small shoulder pads, creates a more refined silhouette. A little bit of extra elegance.
- **Hemline Refinement:** Hem lengths should be chosen with precision—mid-calf can be elegant, while just below the knee is universally flattering. For the most polished look, have the hemline adjusted to fall at the most flattering part of your leg.
- **Lining Alterations:** If a dress clings too much, a tailor can replace the lining with a higher-quality, more breathable fabric for better drape and comfort.
- **Sleeve Length Adjustments:** Shortening long sleeves slightly or adding a slight taper, can create a more elegant line without overwhelming the arms.

Key Tailoring Adjustments for Skirts:

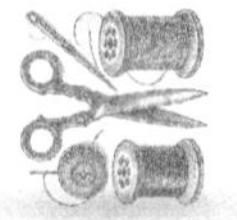

- **Waistband Adjustments:** Many skirts can be tailored at the waistband for a perfect fit. A well-fitted waist ensures that the skirt sits properly on the body without sagging or digging in.
- **Side Seam Refinement:** Skirts should skim the body, not cling or gape—side seams can be subtly taken in, or let out for a custom fit.
- **Hemline Precision:** The right hemline can make or break a skirt. Midi skirts should hit at the slimmest part of the calf for the most flattering effect.
- **Slit Adjustments:** If a slit is too high or too low, a tailor can modify it to enhance comfort and add a little bit of refinement.

Hourglass, pear shaped or athletic, are just general terms: celebrate your physique, and use little tailoring tweaks to create more comfort and ease every day.

Petites: Styling/Tailoring/Adjustments

- Choose long, lean coats. *Ideally look for single breasted, and a mall neat lapel.*
- Structured handheld bags *(oversize hobos weigh smallish people down making them look even smaller.)*
- Draw the eye upwards *with a pair of* stylish earrings, *and aim to create a neat neckline. Avoid anything that draws the eye down, heavy statement shoes for example...*
- Dress tonally. *A light blue shirt with similar tone blue jeans, or a taupe sweater with a brown skirt. Mix textures in the same colour family. Light blue silk, navy wool, dark denim and ocean blue suede. Elongates the silhouette.*
- 3/4 length sleeves—*lovely for those with slim wrists.*
- Comfortable rubber soled boots *(but not over the knee.)*
- Ankle length trousers—*especially suited for those with blessed with slim ankles. Lucky you!*
- Try shoes with a small heel and pointy toes for special occasions *(pointy toes elongate the figure, just make sure they don't pinch).*
- Match the colour of your shoes to your trousers/tights *to create uninterrupted lines.*
- Try cropped jackets with high waisted trousers *this will make legs look longer...much, much longer!*
- Avoid colour blocking *too much colour contrast may cut the silhouette in unflattering places.*

Wardrobe Tailoring know how

Some tweaks—like hemming trousers or nipping in a waist—are easy magic. Others—like fixing a poor fit in the shoulders—are a siren call best resisted. Old Money style wisdom says: know when a garment can be saved and when it's simply not worth the battle.

✅ Good signs (easy to tailor):

Shoulders fit well (especially for jackets and coats)
Shoulder alterations are very expensive and rarely turn out perfectly. **Always** buy jackets, blazers, and structured garments that fit your shoulders properly.

The garment is slightly too big (not too small)
It's easier and cleaner to take garments in than to let them out. Extra fabric can be removed, but it's rare to have enough seam allowance to add width.

Simple hemlines and seams
If you can spot a clean seam (no intricate beading, no heavy lining or embroidery), it's an easier and cheaper fix.

Natural fabrics (cotton, wool, linen, silk)
Tailors find natural fabrics easier to work with. Stretchy synthetics or very slippery fabrics can be more difficult and may not hold alterations as well.

🚫 Warning signs (expensive or risky to tailor):
Shoulders don't fit (too wide or too narrow)
Major shoulder adjustments can distort the entire garment. If the shoulders are off, it's best to leave it.

Garment is too tight all over
Without a visible, generous seam allowance, letting out a piece is often impossible.

Complex designs (beading, ruching, pleats, heavy lining)
The more details and layers, the more expensive and complicated the alteration.

Cheaply made clothing with poor construction
Sometimes inexpensive garments aren't worth tailoring – you may end up spending more on alterations than the piece itself is worth to you.

Elegant Tip: Carry a small measuring tape and a note pad with your measurements shopping. Perfect tailoring can make inexpensive pieces look exquisitely bespoke.

Casual Daily Dressing & Elegance Over 50

Every woman needs a simple yet effective formula to get dressed with ease while looking her very best.

As we refine our wardrobe, comfort and quality become non-negotiable, ensuring that our clothing fits not just our lifestyle but also our changing body needs and climate conditions.

Denim: classic & tailored

You have probably amassed a fair collection of jeans by now: Have a good look to see what you still enjoy wearing and let go of the surplus. A well-fitting pair of jeans is wardrobe joy, but an ill-fitting pair is just clutter. It's nice to have two pairs of denim trousers—one in a dark wash, the other slightly faded for a more relaxed feel. If trousers aren't your preference, consider a fitted denim midi skirt, an equally elegant and modern option. High-quality, 100% cotton denim will hold its shape and last far longer than stretchy alternatives.

Denim is one of the easiest fabrics to source second-hand, often at a fraction of the cost. However, be prepared to rely on the **quiet luxury secret weapon: tailoring.** Buying jeans slightly larger and having them expertly fitted at the waist and hem will elevate them to perfection. The cost of alterations may exceed the price of the jeans themselves, but the result is worthwhile. If you need to shorten a pair, save the excess fabric—it can be repurposed into a bespoke belt or clutch bag for a cohesive, polished look. (*See resources PDF at the end*).

Denim Tips:

- **Dark washes** offer the most versatility.
- **No artificial distressing**—a bit of wear is fine, but avoid 'just been mauled by a tiger' rips.
- **Tailored fit** at the waist, skimming, ideally not touching over the hips, and hemmed to the right length for your footwear.
- **Avoid skinny jeans** they are not particularly comfortable.
- **100% cotton**—no elastane, as it loses shape quickly.

Shirts & T-Shirts: the perfect pairings

Linen, cotton, or silk-blend T-shirts are a breathable, refined choice. They are best tried on in-store first, but once you know your preferred fit, ordering online should be relatively reliable.

For an elevated everyday 'uniform', opt for a few polo shirts with collars or simple Henley tops. Stick to neutral tones initially—charcoal, navy, black, ecru, or bottle green—as they offer longevity and quiet sophistication. While nothing rivals a crisp white shirt, be mindful of its maintenance. If you prefer a lower-maintenance option, consider jersey shirts, which require minimal ironing while maintaining finesse.

Shirts & T-Shirts Tips:

- **Natural fibres only**—100% linen, cotton, or a silk blend.
- No polyester. Ever.
- Collared tops exude quiet luxury.
- Shoulder fit is paramount.
- Stick to neutral hues or classic stripes—no florals at this stage.
- If you opt for cotton or linen, commit to ironing. Otherwise choose a low maintenance jersey piece.

Knitwear:
cozy, chic & timeless

Unless you live somewhere exceptionally hot, knitwear is a quiet luxury staple. A simple V-neck or crew-neck sweater in washable, high-quality wool or good cashmere is a smart foundational piece. Quality lambswool is a better choice than cheap cashmere.

Rollnecks add an 'old-money' touch, but can accentuate double chins and are best suited to colder climates. Cardigans, often unfairly maligned, are both practical and elegant. The key is to style them well—wear one over a matching linen T-shirt for a coordinated look, or drape it effortlessly over your shoulders for a touch of Parisian chic.

Classic Luxury Knitwear Choices (with a touch of the 'old money aesthetic' very quiet luxury!):

1. **Argyle**: A timeless, refined diamond pattern, often in Scottish wools.
2. **Aran**: Beautifully textured Irish sweaters with intricate cable designs.
3. **Fair Isle**: Traditional Shetland patterns, always in style and often reimagined by luxury brands.

Quality knitwear is an investment, it deserves to be cared for with love and attention.

Long Lasting Knitwear Care :

- Wear over a clean base layer (a silk camisole or linen T-shirt).
- Allow wool & cashmere to air between wears.
- Use a steamer or hang in a steamy bathroom to refresh.
- Hand wash or use a gentle machine cycle, then dry flat.
- Store in cashmere bags with cedar wood or lavender essential oil to prevent moth damage.

Coats & outerwear: the definitive power piece

If there's one item worth splurging on, it's a top-quality coat. In colder climates, your coat is the first impression you make—your entire outfit is the coat!

If you live somewhere cold, seek out a long coat in double-faced wool/cashmere or alpaca. Or a lined version with a silk lining for an exquisite finish. If a new designer coat is out of budget, consider a second-hand luxury option, check with your tailor beforehand that it can be expertly altered to fit like a couture piece.

It should be sized large enough to be comfortable over layers or even over a lightweight puffer jacket.

For long walks and outdoor pursuits a waxed, Barbour style jacket is very Old Money. Just add pearls!

Coat Tips

- Avoid pastel or white coats (impractical unless you have a driver and no pets).
- Not too much polyester blends—cheap fabrics degrade quickly.
- 100% cashmere—beautiful, but may prove too delicate for daily wear.

A well-made coat will last 7 years, or more, making the cost per wear (CPW) incredibly worthwhile.

Blazers: the Quiet Luxury essential

Boy-ish blazers and Chanel style jackets may not be daily wear for all, but they are very quiet luxury. A perfectly tailored blazer sets a 'high tone', as it elevates denim, can be layered over a simple dress, and can even add elegance to athleisure wear, even leggings.

A tweed jacket with a silk lining is ideal for traveling and offers temperature regulation while projecting quiet sophistication. If you're unsure whether blazers suit your lifestyle, start with one pre-loved option—wear it and see how it integrates into your wardrobe. Should you find it indispensable, you could always consider a bespoke version later on.

Over the years, fashions evolve, definitely worth adjusting them a little bit to look more contemporary. A good jacket shouldn't be too fitted. (That was the fashion a few years ago.) Nor should it be ludicrously oversized! The modern tweed blazer is boyish, cut loose, and comfortable. It should indent at the waist very slightly to avoid boxiness, but not in any exaggerated way. A strong shoulderline with just a little bit of padding, it helps keep the silhouette neat and slim looking, even though the overall impression is slightly masculine. You really want the shoulders to be just a fraction wider than your shoulder, definitely no huge overhang! That's for the catwalk, not real life.

Blazer Checklist:

- Shoulders must fit perfectly—always.
- Full range of movement is key—you should be able to lift your arms and wave them around!
- Houndstooth, pinstripes, Prince of Wales and checks patterns are very much in keeping with Quiet Luxury.
- Try turning up the collar...
- A single starter blazer is enough to refine your wardrobe.

Fewer, Better Pieces

Dressing with quiet luxury over 50 is about editing your wardrobe to contain only the best-fitting, most flattering pieces. Two tailored pairs of jeans, a lovely dress, a beautifully cut blazer, and a luxurious coat will do more for your style than a closet full of trendy, ill-fitting garments. Quality over quantity, always.

That Dress:
easiest of Quiet Luxury pieces

We've touched on dresses before, but they deserve another mention. The right dress is effortless—something you can slip on and instantly look beautifully put together. No fuss, no overthinking. A long cashmere jumper dress or a crisp cotton shirt dress—wear it and go, effortless style in a nutshell!

Timeless & Effortless Options

1. **Wrap Dresses**–Universally flattering and easy to tailor for a perfect fit. Solid colours are so versatile.
2. **Sheath Dresses**–Skims the body without clinging, Such a refined silhouette.
3. **Shirt Dresses**–Classic and practical, worn loose or cinched with a belt. Different belts change the look!
4. **Knit Dresses**–For cold weather elegance, nothing like a soft cashmere/merino wool knit! It feels as luxurious as it looks. Avoid those with cling.
5. **Flowing Silk or Linen Dresses**–Light, breathable, and elegant, (luxury billowy sleeves allowing the skin to breathe).

The beauty of these pieces is their simplicity. No unnecessary details—only the best natural fabrics, simple cuts, and the quiet confidence of knowing you're well dressed with minimal effort.

Quality control for key pieces

Should I buy a fast fashion silk shirt (example: MANGO or Lily Silk 100% silk satin or choose the pricier more upmarket version (example: 100 % silk georgette from Theory)? They are both in natural fabrics and they both look very gorgeous on line.

It is worth allocating some time to check these items in person, but here is a comparative overview.

The **silk georgette shirt from Theory** will generally look more elegant than the **silk satin shirt from Mango** for a few key reasons:

1. **Fabric Quality & Drape**–Theory's silk georgette has a soft, matte texture with a refined, slightly sheer quality, creating an effortlessly luxurious look. It drapes beautifully and feels understated yet sophisticated. In contrast, silk satin, especially from a high-street brand like Mango, or Lilysilk, can sometimes appear overly shiny or synthetic, which can look less refined.
2. **Cut & Fit**–Theory is known for its superior tailoring and minimalist, high-end aesthetic. Their silk georgette shirts will likely have a better fit and finish, elevating the overall appearance. Mango, being more trend-driven and mass-market, may not offer the same level of polish. Lilysilk tailoring is usually hit and miss.
3. **Versatility & Timelessness**–A silk georgette shirt is more versatile; its subtle elegance makes it perfect for

both day and evening wear without looking too formal. A silk satin shirt, depending on the sheen, can sometimes read as more occasion-specific or even slightly cheap if the finish isn't quite right.

If the goal is quiet luxury, the Theory silk georgette shirt is the better choice—it exudes effortless refinement without trying too hard.

Silk satin shirt with jeans & pearls–where to wear It:

Using the example of denim here to keep the look relatively relaxed and casual. A silk satin shirt with jeans and pearls creates a polished yet somewhat glamorous look. The sheen of the fabric makes it best suited for occasions that call for a bit of sophistication but aren't overly formal.We are partial to a dash of rose or cream silk satin as it throws a very flattering hue on the skin. Beautifully suited for:

1. **Upscale Brunch or Afternoon Tea**–A silk satin blouse with denim, delicate pearls, and elegant flats or kitten heels is perfect for a refined but relaxed setting. Wonderful just peeking out of a v-neck sweater for a care free vibe.
2. **Dinner at a Stylish Restaurant**–The subtle sheen elevates the look for a nice dinner without being overdressed. Adding a tailored blazer takes it to a whole new level of chic.

3. **Cocktail Hour**–Satin catches the light beautifully in the evening, making it a great choice for a chic, casual drinks event.
4. **Gallery Openings or Cultural Events**–The luxurious fabric contrasts well with the relaxed denim, striking the perfect balance between elegance and effortlessness.
5. **Date Night (definitely Effortless but Elegant)**–satin's natural glow enhances the skin, making it an ideal choice for a softly sophisticated yet approachable look.

Silk georgette shirt with jeans & pearls – where to wear it:

On the other hand a silk georgette shirt has a more understated elegance, with a matte, slightly sheer texture that makes it more versatile for day-to-evening wear.

1. **Work Meetings or Business Casual Settings**–The subtle elegance of georgette makes it a great option for a professional look, especially with a structured blazer.
2. **Casual Chic for Weekend Outings**–Whether strolling through a charming old town or having coffee in a beautiful café, the fabric's drape gives off effortless sophistication. Satin may appear as a little 'too much in those settings.
3. **Museum or Bookstore Visits**–The refined quality of georgette works well for intellectual or cultural outings, paired with well-cut jeans and classic loafers.

4. **Travel Days (Luxurious but Comfortable)**–Unlike satin, georgette resists creasing, making it a smart choice for elegant but practical travel attire.
5. **Informal Gatherings with a Stylish Crowd**– f the setting is relaxed but filled with people who appreciate style, (your bookclub for example) the georgette shirt blends elegance with ease.

The Verdict:

- Satin is slightly dressier and works well for evening or semi-formal occasions.
- Georgette is more refined and subtle, perfect for daytime elegance and effortless chic.

Both are a good wardrobe investment—it just depends on budget, the mood and setting!

Going forward, the same thought process can be applied to all your key purchases. The quiet luxury woman, takes her time before reaching for the credit card. There is absolutely no hint of rush or desperation.

The Role of Accessories in Elevating Your Look

Too much jewellery can look dated, and pilling on statement accessories appears cumbersome and artificial. Avoid the 'trying too hard vibe'. Light touch is what we need here!

By the time we are 50 we might have realised that knowing what to leave out is just as important as knowing what to wear.
Accessorising at this point needs a light hand. However, the accessories themselves probably need to be of the very best quality you can afford. Vintage and 'faux bijou' most definitely have place in the discerning wardrobe, but they need to be exquisitely made! More vintage Dior and less Primark.

jewellery

18 carat gold chain

This needs to be simple in design and the very best quality. Definitely nothing with overt branding. It looks lovely gleaming over a navy sweater or peeking under a crisp shirt collar. Or even layered with a pearl necklace, or another gold pendant. Three pendants maximum! Your local jeweller might have some good options to try for the most versatile length, that suits your neckline.

pearl necklace

If you are the classic pearl necklace type, it's easy to style. It doesn't even have to be real pearls, vintage glass pearls look stunning and can be bought from eBay for a song. Say no to the contemporary plastic pearls and look for good quality 'faux' from the 60s 70s and 80s. (Look for vintage 'lotus' pearls) Graduated pearls, princess style pearls and maybe a longer sautoir or opera length. Pearls look their best when paired with something more up to date, to avoid looking like a dated cliché.

Gold, diamond & pearl clip ons & studs

The size of your earrings can have a big impact on how facial features appear. Larger earrings tend to suit mature faces and can balance out a prominent nose creating a striking, beautiful look. (Avoid heavy earrings that pull the ear lobe though!) No substitute for trying things on! Smaller studs look the most elegant and diamonds should be discreetly small but super sparkly. (FL) Definitively not large and dull. Lab grown faux and zirconium are perfectly acceptable options; if one gets misplaced, not a huge loss.

'Faux' bijoux

Seek out vintage, clip-on earrings. Vintage D'Orlan Swarovski, Dior, Givenchy or Trifari costume clip-ons (*request resources PDF*) Large earrings can look absolutely magnificent as statement pieces when worn on their own with no other jewellery! Quality vintage gold plated jewellery, crystal earrings, sparkly brooches or necklaces, yes even lucite or plastic ones, are fun additions, as long as they are of the very best quality. Always use with restraint. To keep it Quiet Luxury just the ONE statement piece per outfit.

Contemporary designers

If you are able to support small contemporary designers, very modern jewellery often pairs well with classic clothing. It allows your discerning taste to shine, keeping the outfit current and relevant.

Non-negotiable when it comes to jewellery

- Yes to vintage and antique, 18ct gold.
- Look for Realistic looking (but 'faux') pearls & diamonds, delicate looking rather than improbably huge.
- Avoid cliché, branded jewellery as trending on instagram. Alhambra for example, or worse those semi-illegal Alhambra copies.

It is also worth a look into auctions and only buy things you really love rather than what everyone else has.

scarves

Silk carré

The late Queen Elizabeth of England had a huge collection of Hermès silks —which she wore casually. There are many pictures of her wearing them at the races or when enjoying the outdoors in her country walks. Scarves go in and out of fashion—but a silk carré (square around 70 or 90 cm) is a wardrobe staple that will add joyful colour and pattern into a plain monochromatic outfit. Simply choose colours that you love and don't worry too much about coordination or complicated knots. The Quiet Luxury woman wears her scarves around the neck, tied to a handbag, or used as a headscarf à la Grace Kelly. Just not all at the same time!

A couple of fun 'how to' illustrations borrowed from the Hermès knotting cards for inspiration! Make a bag with your scarf, tie your silk scarf round your head on bad hair days or use one round the neck for that aristocratic 'Old Money' chic. To keep the silk scarf look 'nonchalant 'choose a simple method and practice it until you achieve perfection.It can be quite meditative!

If you buy a scarf directly from Hermès boutiques they are usually only too delighted to show you different ways to wear them.

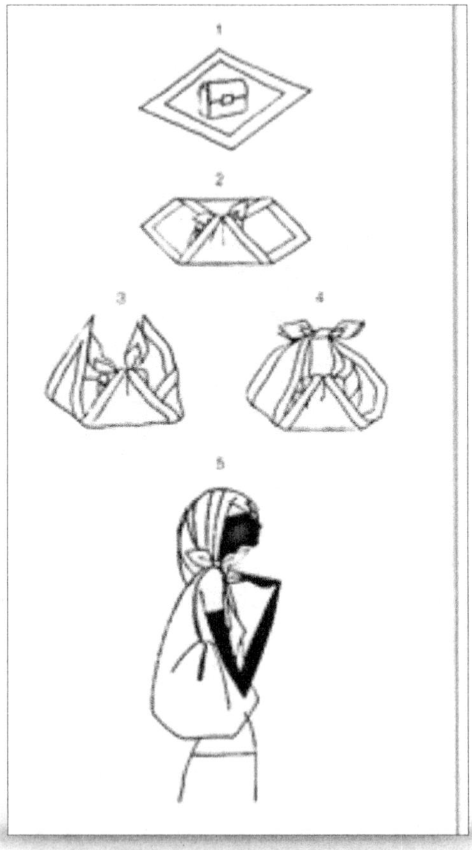
1
2
3
4
5

Cashmere Scarves:

In cold weather nothing feels more luxurious than a generous cashmere scarf. It adds warmth and finishes off an outfit to a higher standard. The scarf needs to be big enough to make you feel enveloped, and drape with elegance, nothing skimpy will do.
The best quality cashmere is made in Scotland or Italy. This is one item where it is worth paying a little extra. Do ensure the colour you choose compliment your favourite daily coat or jacket.

gloves

Leather or cashmere gloves are a lovely addition to any well-rounded Quiet Luxury accessories collection. Black or brown are a practical choice for the colder months adding a polished finish to your outfit. Don't dismiss bright colours though: chartreuse, cerise or peacock blue can add a bright, luxurious hue to a plain outfit. Cashmere-lined gloves are pure indulgence, but they also offer extra warmth.

belts

Leather Belts

You probably have a lot of belts by now, acquired over the years. Clear out the cheap looking ones and only keep the best examples. Sturdy leather and attractive buckles. One doesn't actually need a lot of belts, a black brown and a tan should cover most eventualities. If you wear a statement necklace or earrings do make sure the belt buckle is simple and doesn't fight visually. Likewise if you have a very beautiful buckle - treat it like jewellery.

Fabric Belts:

A self-fabric belt can be custom-made from fabric remnants. For instance, if you've had a dress or a pair of jeans tailored, you can use the leftover fabric to create a matching belt. These belts offer a thoughtfully coordinated, yet casual, look—perfect for the Quiet Luxury aesthetic. Custom belts in your own fabric can often be made at a surprisingly affordable price point. (*See my PDF resources.*)

shoes

The Quiet Luxury' style wardrobe includes a well-curated (and sometimes excessive) collection of shoes. Leave out ugly orthopaedic looking shoes. There is really no need! Comfort, as well as elegance can be found in contemporary trainers, plimsols, and simple leather loafers.
It is best if we only wear shoes that we can walk in for at least an hour. Comfort takes precedence! A well-made, pair of trainers or moccasins has become an acceptable everyday choice—even in the most refined circles. Look after your shoes, it makes all the difference: keep them scrupulously clean, rotate pairs to prevent odour & wear, and add leather insoles if synthetics don't appeal.

Consider coordinating your trainers with your outfit, much like the old rule about matching shoes to a belt. Matching your leather shoes to your belt is still a nice touch, *but* avoid matching the handbag as well. Two matching things is good, three may be 'too much'.

Shoes that support posture & poise
If at all possible make walking part of your healthy lifestyle and wear shoes to support daily walks. Good footwear contributes to good posture, so don't neglect them. If you have serious foot problems, bunions and the like, visit a podiatrist for advice. Wide-fitting shoes may be a better option, nowadays there is a lot of choice. (*see resources PDF*)
A well chosen pair of shoes promotes balance, while badly designed ones can lead to misery, discomfort and long term damage to your body. Avoid most sky high heels, any tight shoes that squeeze the toes, and what we call "shuffling shoes"–styles that require a gripping or dragging motion to stay on, such as pool slides, crocs, or flip-flops. They hinder graceful movement.

For a refined but still practical wardrobe, consider:

- **Trainers**–Clean, well-maintained pairs for easy everyday wear and lots of healthy walking. Several pairs in different colours.
- **Loafers & Moccasins**–Polished yet comfortable, easy to slip on for errands or casual outings. One or two pairs.
- **Ballet Flats**–Timeless and elegant, though not always the most supportive for long walks. They don't suit everyone and feel free to skip them altogether.
- **Mid to Low-Heeled Pumps**–The go-to for formal occasions, ensuring both comfort and sophistication. Pointed heel elongates the leg, but avoid anything than pinches the poor toes (ouch!).

For **special events**, opt for classic pumps in leather or satin—but choose them only after selecting your outfit to ensure some level of coordination.

For **outdoor practicality**, a pair of wellington boots in dark green, black, or a playful colour works for truly muddy environments. Flip-flops? Strictly for the beach only. A quiet luxury woman always takes a moment to change into the appropriate footwear before heading to lunch or dinner. Never goes to lunch wearing flip-flops.

You may want to clear out your closet from too many old pairs of shoes, no matter how expensive they once were. Quiet Luxury is having the space and being able to see what you have!

clear out your closet from too many old pairs of shoes, no matter how expensive they once were.

Glasses & sunglasses

Reading Glasses: style meets function
By midlife, most women require reading glasses, making them a daily necessity. Pay attention to them otherwise they are a missed opportunity—**elegant, well-fitted frames** can be as stylish as any other well chosen fashion accessory.

- **Invest in Multiple Pairs**–keep one in your handbag, one at your desk, and another by your bedside to avoid frantic searching.
- **Find a Signature Frame**–whether it's a chic tortoiseshell, understated wire rims, or soft cat-eye lenses, well-chosen frames flatter the face and enhance your overall aesthetic.

Glasses—whether for reading or sun protection—should be **intentional, not an afterthought.** Consider how they look with your hair, earrings, neckline or scarf. A quiet luxury woman knows that thoughtful, small details make a large impact.

Sunglasses: statement & discretion
The right pair of sunglasses can instantly elevate any look, lending an air of effortless sophistication. Try a few pairs on before you decide. Cats-eye almost aways looks sophisticated and just a little oversize is fine. Not ludicrously big though. **Choosing quality over Logos**—timeless frames with proper UV protection. A discreet monogram may be acceptable, but large, flashy branding is not in keeping with quiet luxury. Do remove your sunglasses when speaking with someone. Making eye contact and offering a warm, affable smile is a simple yet powerful way to exude presence and charm. Nothing says quiet confidence like engaging fully with those around us.

Instant style: always accessorise with the mystery of sunglasses, immaculately clean shoes and your favourite handbag

Handbags

A lovely handbag is a sophisticated finishing touch, however we are not fooled: there is no magic handbag to save a poorly put together ensemble.

What to do with old handbags?

By the time a woman reaches her 50s, she has likely collected a lifetime of handbags—some classic, some dated, and some that no longer align with her current quiet luxury aesthetic. So, what to do with them?

1. Should You Still Use Them?

Absolutely! Some well-made, older bags may even feel more luxurious over time, developing a beautiful patina and a soft, lived-in elegance. However, certain styles may need a rethink.

- Classic, timeless designs (structured leather bags, simple totes, or quality cross-body purses) can still be used with confidence, provided they are simple.
- Logo-heavy or overly trendy pieces can sometimes be reworked, but if they feel dated or don't reflect your aesthetic anymore, it might be time to part with them. It is far more luxurious to have the space and curate your belongings!
- Heavy, oversized bags can feel cumbersome—switching to lighter-weight styles might just refresh your look.

2. How to Refresh and Restyle Old Bags

If you still love the shape and quality of a bag but it feels outdated, a few styling tricks can bring it back to life:

- Add a silk scarf–Tying a beautiful scarf around the handle can instantly elevate and soften the look. Perhaps even a (high quality) fun bag charm!
- Use a bag insert–Helps reshape slouchy bags and give them some much needed structure.
- Restyle how you carry it–A structured handbag held lightly in the hand (rather than overstuffed and slung over the shoulder) looks more elegant.
- Polish or condition leather–A little care can bring older bags back to life. There are specialist places that can do that for you. While you are there recondition your shoes as well. (*see resources*)

3. Repurpose, Gift, or Sell

For bags that no longer fit your style but are still in good condition:

- Sell them–Consignment stores and online platforms (*Vestiaire Collective, The RealReal are just two examples, look into local ones*) can help them find a new home.
- Gift to a younger friend or relative–A niece or daughter may love a well-crafted vintage bag. However be mindful not to force it on them.
- Repurpose them–A smaller clutch bag could be turned into an elegant cosmetic pouch, pencil case or beautiful organiser.

4. When to Let Go

If a bag is too worn, impractical, or no longer brings you joy, you know the answer: it's time to declutter. A quiet luxury wardrobe isn't about hoarding pieces just because they were expensive—it's about curating collections that truly work.

A woman over 50 has earned the right to refine her collection—keeping only the pieces that enhance her style, simplify her life, and make her feel relevant as well as elegant.

When to buy a new handbag?

Any time that you feel like cheering up? After all the handbag always fits, even on 'bad hair' days. Seriously though, should you buy a new handbag every season, every year? When your old bag feels a bit tatty perhaps? Or simply keep buying till you can no longer shut the door of your closet, and you have to stuff your handbags under the bed?

The answer to that is very personal, but in reality a well-rounded handbag collection need only consist of four or five pieces, even if you are an influencer!'

A well-chosen handbag is a **finishing touch**, rather than the foundation of a stylish ensemble—it's about selecting **functional, beautifully made** bags that enhance an outfit within the context of our lifestyle.

Example of a Quiet Luxury handbag collection

The Large Tote

Perfect choice to be prepared for every eventuality. You carry everything you could possibly need with room to spare: sandwiches, home-made snacks, iPad, several pairs of glasses, umbrella, keys, vitamins, cosmetic pouch ... practical, everyday bag! While a structured leather tote is the classic choice, it can be heavy. A lightweight cotton or canvas tote could make for an elegant, understated alternative carry all, minus the weight. Keep it scrupulously clean though, as an added bonus canvas bags are usually less inexpensive.

The Handheld Structured Bag

Smart and (and quite literally) polished, this bag complements tailored coats and blazers without disrupting the clean lines of impeccable tailoring. It can also elevate more casual denim outfits for a bit of contrast. Ideal for coffee dates, luncheons, gallery openings...so very chic!

The Small Crossbody

Perfect for hands-free ease while traveling, walking the dogs or running errands. A sleek, minimal design ensures it remains elegant, **not bulky**. Avoid overly complicated convertible bags—you know the sort too many zips, to many compartments, simplicity is key.

The Summer Basket Bag

This is really the summery version of the leather hold all: Structured straw or raffia bag brings effortless charm to summer outfits. Ideal for **informal garden parties, beach trips, or alfresco lunches**. Adding a favourite silk scarf to the handle can elevate and create more personality and a signature look..

The Clutch Bag

Master the art of carrying a neat little clutch with finesse. Practice at home if need be! Ideally, a clutch matches the colour of an evening dress and is made from coordinated satin or velvet fabric. However something in **gold, silver, or a bejewelled minaudière** is a glamorous alternative.

If you like the minimal elegance of carrying a clutch, include one in leather or good quality straw to be used casually during the day. It needs to be large enough to carry your essentials: reading glasses, keys, phone, maybe a lip balm. The epitome of effortless chic.

Luggage: traveling with Quiet Luxury

You are cosmopolitan quiet luxury woman who treats her luggage as an extension of her wardrobe. Refined and practical with no overt branding.

- **A high-quality rolling suitcase** or even a matching set for frequent travellers. Smaller cases for weekend getaways, larger ones for longer trips. Durable polycarbonate—lightweight yet robust enough for frequent use. Vintage leather is lovely but too heavy and impractical for the demands of modern travel.
- **A simple weekend bag** in soft leather or structured canvas, perfect for short trips and carry-on travel.
- **A compact travel backpack**, elegant yet functional, offering hands-free convenience. It can be a little rugged to tell stories of past voyages, but kept clean!

Packing cubes are a relatively recent phenomena, yet invaluable for organising clothes, shoes and travel essentials in a suitcase or carry on. Packing with intention and thoughtfully selecting light, versatile luggage ensures every journey is a stylish pleasure.

Your Style Evolution cheat sheet: elegance over 50

A Guide for the Woman Over 50 to Refine Her Wardrobe with Quiet Luxury & Old Money Elegance

A woman's style naturally evolves with time, and after 50, it's about curating a wardrobe that reflects confidence, refinement, and effortless sophistication. Focusing on quality over quantity, impeccable tailoring, and timeless elegance. investing in pieces that exude grace and understated wealth.

✔ **Investing just like aristocrats and 'old money'**– Only buy a few pieces, but the very best you can afford.

✔ **Luxurious fabrics**–organic cotton, linen, hemp, silk, quality wool, breathe well in menopause and beyond.

✔ **Finding a tailor**–or a local seamstress you can trust. A few clever adjustments to improve fit can elevate even the simplest of outfits to the epitome of chic.

✔ **Classic Neutrals**–choose one or two colours to create the foundation of your wardrobe: Camel, navy, grey, ivory, and chocolate brown.

✔ **Colourful Accents**–add your favourite colour in small doses. Emerald, burgundy, pink, French blue...

✔ **Effortless Dressing**–create an easy 'uniform' for daily chic. Signature looks (e.g., silk blouse + tailored denim) simplify style.

✔ **Refined Accessories**–one or two pieces of jewellery, structured leather bags, silk scarves to add polish.

✔ **Comfortable Footwear**–loafers, refined sneakers, and classic boots ensure comfort & sophistication. Walk as much as possible to stay fit and healthy.

✔ **Beauty & Health Basics**–well looked after skin, soft makeup, clean nails and beautifully maintained hair to complete the look. Exercise is now part of daily life.

✔ **Seasonal fine-tuning**–every season assess and update your wardrobe to align with your lifestyle.

✔ **Acknowledge Privilege of age**–refinement comes with age, at this stage in life—true beauty lies in wisdom, presence and kindness.

Luxurious options: Dressing for Any Occasion

Let's look at some classic scenarios where the quiet luxury fashion choices are allowed to shine. Everyday refinement, a little bit of evening wear, travel elegance, and of course, special events.

Nephew's Basketball Game

A quiet luxury woman over 50 has the wisdom to know that even casual outings is an opportunity for effortless elegance. A sports day or basketball game calls for comfort, practicality, and understated style, without resorting to sloppy athleisure.

A crisp linen or cotton button-down shirt, its sleeves casually rolled up, pairs perfectly with comfortable chinos or high-waisted straight-leg jeans—structured yet relaxed. If there's a chill in the air, we layer with a fine-knit cashmere sweater or a lightweight quilted gilet, ensuring practicality without compromising style.

Chic sneakers provide comfort for walking across the field or navigating stadium steps, while a structured crossbody bag or a sleek tote keeps her essentials close at hand. Minimal accessories—perhaps a classic wristwatch, understated gold earrings, and a slim leather belt—add polish without fuss. For outdoor events, she might complete the look with chic sunglasses and a fun baseball cap! Here we are: exuding a quiet confidence that makes even the most casual occasions feel refined.

Wedding Guest

A well-cut midi or tea-length silk dress in a timeless shade—soft dove grey, French navy, or an elegant blush—these colours always look calm and sophisticated. Weather is often unpredictable so be well prepared with a lightweight coat or a cashmere shawl in a coordinated shade. It doesn't have to match exactly, but it needs to look considered.

Jewellery is chosen with a light hand—perhaps an heirloom pearl necklace or some bold earrings. Perhaps a cocktail ring, but definitely not all of the above, go with 'less is more'.

Footwear is both chic and comfortable, with elegant mid-heel pumps or kitten heels in neutral tones. Handbags are usually structured and discreet, maybe a sleek clutch in satin or smooth leather—prominent logos and excess embellishments have no place here.

If the wedding is formal, a natty little hat or a beautifully crafted fascinator adds an air of sophistication, effortlessly complementing the overall ensemble. The look is polished, graceful, and most importantly, always appropriate.

Going to yoga class

It should come as no surprise that the Quiet Luxury woman is keen on her yoga or pilates class. A weekly session if she can fit it in, but also regular online zoom classes in between. How else would she look so good in her quiet luxury outfits?

High-quality activewear in soft, neutral tones—breathable leggings and a sleek, moisture-wicking tank top. She prefers organic cotton rather than polyester, because it feels so much better against the skin. Layering with a zip-up jacket over her shoulders, ensuring both warmth and elegance before and after the yoga class.

She has her own mat neatly tucked into a discreet, stylish carrier. Minimalist sneakers or slip-on ballet flats complete the look, while a small tote carries her water bottle, silk scrunchie, and an organic face mist for a post-class refresh. Needless to say she only wears yoga pants for actual yoga. She moves with ease, embodying grace that define quiet luxury at any age.

Grandchildren's School Concert

For a quiet luxury woman over 50, attending a school concert is about striking the perfect balance between effortless elegance and relaxed comfort. She wants to look polished yet approachable—never overdressed, that would embarrass the kids!

A cashmere turtleneck or a fine merino wool sweater in a soft, flattering hue (think camel, dove grey, or navy) pairs beautifully with tailored trousers, dark wash jeans or a chic midi skirt.

If the event is particularly informal, she may opt for the dark-wash, well-fitted jeans—but always paired with a structured blazer or a timeless wool coat to maintain a sense of occasion. Make he grandkids proud!

For footwear, comfort is always at the front of our mind. Low-heeled ankle boots, elegant leather loafers, or even trainers ensure chic with ease of movement. A neat little tote handbag—large enough to carry a small gift or flowers for the grandchild's performance—completes the look.

Jewellery is minimal yet thoughtful—perhaps a delicate gold chain, a classic pair of pearl studs, and her signature wristwatch.

This outfit is the embodiment of quiet confidence and timeless grace—an ensemble that shows she's put together without trying too hard. The sort of woman that looks as beautifully elegant in the school auditorium just as she would in even the grandest of the grand opera-house settings!

Charity Dinner & Dance

Glamorous charity events do sometimes multiply as we get older. And if they don't, we could simply create them and host them ourselves in our own home. What to wear? Depending on formality, start with a structured, knee-length or full-length dress in an opulent fabric—think silk crepe, velvet, or a fine wool blend—that makes a good foundation for a glamorous evening look. Colours can be rich yet stay refined: deep emerald, classic navy, or a shade of champagne.

A matching silk coat or a cashmere wrap adds refinement as well as being practical, to ensure warmth without sacrificing elegance. Generally we steer away from excessive matchy-matchiness, but this is one occasion we can go all out!

Jewellery can include an art deco brooch, a vintage cuff bracelet, or elegant drop earrings. This is the right place for the bold cocktail ring or that statement necklace from Boodles or Van Cleef & Arpels.

Elegant evening pumps are the natural choice, ensuring grace with every step. A beautifully crafted minaudière or a small velvet clutch completes the look—discreet, functional, and utterly refined.

Confidence, grace, and quiet opulence!

Travel Elegance

During a long-or short-haul flight the quiet luxury woman thinks about both style and comfort. A soft, breathable cashmere or merino wool wrap layered over a lightweight linen or cotton blouse—perfect for adjusting to the ever changing cabin temperatures and dry air. Freezing one minute, boiling the next! Relaxed fit trousers in a darker neutral tone keep the look polished, while a pair of sleek leather slip-on sneakers ensure ease through airport security. No belts with clunky hardware, they will raise security alarms, causing mayhem. An extra pair of clean socks and a face mask are neatly tacked in her slouchy tote bag. It carries her other travel essentials, including a silk eye mask, a small, hydrating facial mist, her phone and her well-worn leather passport holder. Minimal jewellery—perhaps simple gold hoops or a classic watch—adds just the right amount of refinement.

Effortlessly chic, she boards her flight ready to arrive at her destination in style, with a panama hat neatly rolled in her carry-on!

Beauty & Grooming for Menopause and Beyond

Skincare, haircare, and essential self-care rituals to uplift, soothe and elevate.

The quiet luxury woman knows that self-care isn't about trying to remain frozen in time but about beautifully enhancing her skin, hair, nails—adding radiance, confidence, and elegance. She embraces a simple skin & hair routine that prioritises hydration, nourishment, and overall well-being rather than miracle cures, invasive surgery and quick fixes.

Simple daily skincare, paying attention to a balanced diet, and a lifestyle that supports natural vitality. Beauty at this stage is about refinement.

Skincare: hydration is everything

Mature skin craves moisture, so the focus should be on deeply hydrating serums—look for products containing hyaluronic acid, peptides, and ceramides. A rich but non-greasy moisturiser is essential, and always—always —SPF. Gentle cleansing; avoid harsh foaming cleansers that strip the skin. At night, a few drops of facial oil followed by lymphatic drainage self-massage, gua sha, or face yoga can offer a natural lift—no needles required. Retinol? Sure, but proceed with caution. A low-strength retinol or retinaldehyde used a couple of nights a week can encourage skin renewal without irritation. If skin becomes red and flaky, that's overdoing it—pull back, hydrate, and try again later. Slow and steady wins the radiance race.

When selecting new skincare products, it's advisable to choose formulations with fewer but quality ingredients to reduce the risk of irritation. French Pharmacy brands like Avène offer products with soothing properties to calm and protect sensitive skin, during menopause and beyond. They also offer a wonderful mineral spray, perfect for travel. Additionally, incorporating products free from fragrances and unnecessary additives can be beneficial. Opting for gentle, hydrating cleansers and moisturisers with straightforward ingredient lists can help maintain skin health without triggering sensitivities. If in any doubt, patch-test new products to ensure compatibility with your skin. (r*esources PDF*)

Makeup: soft definition

Quiet Luxury has the ethos of less is more. Whispering rather than shouting. The best makeup is weightless and enhancing, with no heavy layers. A light-reflecting tinted moisturiser evens out the skin without settling into lines. Cream-based blush and highlighter add life to the face. Eyebrows get more sparse with age and usually need some definition. Well-shaped (but not overdrawn) brows to frame the eyes beautifully. Brown rather than black mascara and a flattering, hydrating lip colour is often all that's needed for an effortless, polished look.

Hair: healthy & bouncy

We should not feel the need to cut our hair short just because we are 50 or 60. However long hair does require more time and upkeep so choosing a haircut suitable to hair type and lifestyle is a wise option!

Healthy, well-maintained hair is the signature look for quiet luxury. Dirty, unkempt hair will destroy even the loveliest of outfits. It is unfortunate that hair does become drier with age, but luckily deep conditioning masks, scalp massage, and hair supplements (*like collagen or biotin, see resources*) are excellent investments. Over-processing is the enemy—embrace rich, multi tonal colour rather than solid flat shades. Of course, bad hair days, are a fact of life at any age. The Quiet Luxury woman greets them with a bit of humour as she throws on her beautiful silk scarf with a shrug.

Nails: well-groomed

Neatly trimmed nails—whether short and buffed or with a sheer nude or soft pink polish—exude quiet luxury. Harsh acrylics or overly elaborate nail art feel dated and most definitely not 'quiet luxury'! Regular SPF on your hands as on your face is an excellent habit to get into, the earlier the better. Brittle, peeling nails may respond well to extra vitamin-D supplements. Include a hand cream and some oil application to keep hands looking elegant and beautifully well cared for.

Dental Care: investment smile

Nothing ages a face faster than neglected teeth. Regular visits to the dentist and hygienist are non-negotiable, ensuring a bright, healthy smile. Find a reputable dentist and visit the hygienist at least twice a year. They will usually show you the best brushing technique for your individual needs. Don't overdo the whitening, it is not essential! However it is nice to get rid coffee and red wine stains. Keep it to just one or two shades lighter.

A sound dental routine could be: twice a day brushing, using interdental sticks, drinking water rather than fizzy sodas and daily use of a Ayurvedic copper tongue scraper, (*see resources PDF*). The tongue scraper will help ensure fresher breath enhancing confidence and wellbeing. Quick, inexpensive and effective.

Perfume: the invisible luxury

Ladies go easy on the fragrance. Quiet luxury perfume should feel like a little secret. Light and barely there.

For daytime, fresh scents with soft floral, citrus, or woody notes are good options, nothing too sweet. In the evening, a deeper, more sensual scent with notes of sandalwood, iris, or amber can add quiet allure without overwhelming the room.

Application of perfume is an art in itself: wrists, behind the ears, and the collarbone—or spray it in the air and walk underneath it. A tiny dab on the inside of a freshly laundered coat or scarf allows the scent to linger beautifully. When in doubt, less is always more.

Quiet Luxury beauty cheat sheet for after 50

Daily Essentials

Morning

Cleanse–A splash of water, a gentle cream cleanser or rosewater refreshes skin without stripping.
Hydrate–Layer hyaluronic acid, a nourishing moisturiser with SPF 30+ (yes, even in winter).
Lips & Eyes–A swipe of Vaseline on lips and under eyes keeps hydration locked in.
Minimal Makeup–Tinted moisturiser, whisper of cream blush, softly defined brows, hydrating lip colour.

Throughout the Day

- Keep lips supple with a tinted balm or simple Vaseline.
- Have a water spritz handy, especially in hot weather.
- Reapply SPF if outdoors.
- Drink plenty of water and snack on fresh fruit & nuts for skin benefits and general health.
- Walk with upright posture—instant boost!

Evening

Cleanse–Remove makeup with a delicious milk cleanser or a rich cleansing balm.
Nourish–Apply a quality night cream or facial oil. Include peptides & ceramides when possible.
Face Yoga–A few minutes of massage or gua sha for lymphatic drainage. It will relax and reduce puffiness
Silk Hair Curler–Wrap hair for effortless waves while protecting against breakage.
Silk Satin Pillowcase–Helps skin retain moisture and prevents hair frizz.

Weekly or monthly extras

Skin & Body

- Gentle exfoliation for radiant skin (enzyme-based, no harsh scrubs).
- Long bath with Epsom salts or a sauna session.
- Deep hydration mask for face & body (slather Vaseline on feet & wear socks overnight!).

Hair & Nails

- Deep conditioning hair masque for soft, glossy locks.
- Scalp massage with nourishing oil for stronger hair growth and .
- Eyebrow trim and tint for a naturally polished look.
- Manicure with sheer nude, soft pink, or just a good buff and oil.

Self-Care & Relaxation

- Foot massage or reflexology session.
- Yoga or gentle stretching to maintain posture and flexibility.
- Read something uplifting before bed, (like this book)and minimise screen time!

Every six months

- Visit a dermatologist for a skin health check-up and personalised advice, if required.
- Dental hygienist & check-up—healthy teeth = timeless beauty.
- Reassess skincare & hair products seasonally—upgrade or simplify as needed.

Poise, Posture, the Art of Presence over 50

Carrying Yourself with Grace and Confidence

The quiet luxury woman understands that poise and posture elevate even the simplest outfit. Style is not just about what you wear; it's more about how you move, how you sit, and how you hold yourself. That tailored blazer is only as elegant as the way you wear it, and even the most beautiful silk blouse loses its charm if the wearer is slouching.

While some were fortunate to learn these skills through childhood ballet, equestrian pursuits, or even finishing school etiquette, these are qualities that can be cultivated at any stage of life. Presence is a mindset as much as it is a physical state. However there is no substitute for the discipline of regular exercise, even if its just daily walking. Invaluable to cultivate health, and an appreciation for elegant movement.

The Foundation of Graceful Movement

Fluid silhouettes that skim the body look graceful and convey a sense of ease. That ease can also extend to how you carry yourself.

Posture as a Daily Practice

- Imagine lengthening your spine as though a silk thread were gently pulling you upwards from the crown of your head.
- Keep shoulders relaxed—lift them slightly, then roll them back and down.
- When seated, avoid collapsing into a chair with a thud! Instead, sit with both feet resting on the floor and an engaged yet comfortable posture.
- Avoid stiff, over-rehearsed movements—grace should feel natural, not staged.

Movement that Speaks Elegance

- Channel the grace of a catwalk model (*in a natural way*): slightly overcrossing one foot in front of the other (just don't trip!) creates a fluid, elongated motion that looks effortlessly refined. This technique, sometimes called the 'cat walk,' (all domestic cats naturally walk like that!) prevents clunky, heavy steps and adds grace to your movement.
- Walk with quiet confidence, placing each step with intention. Steady and even is always more refined than rushing.
- Whether wearing ballet flats or boots, opt for supportive shoes that allow you to walk with ease.
- Use your hands gracefully but with control—avoid exaggerated gestures.

Refining Poise Through Mindful Practices

Graceful movement often stems from strong, supple muscles and a centred mind. Yoga, Pilates and Tai Chi practices are well worth pursuing at any stage in life, even more so now!

Yoga: develops strength, flexibility, and balance—ideal for strong core and healthy spine! To maintain elegance, clarity of thought and energy at any age. (*resources PDF*)

Pilates & Dance classes: strengthen the core and refine posture, ensuring that clothing drapes beautifully over a well-aligned frame.

Tai Chi: encourages slow, purposeful movement and balance—perfect for cultivating an unhurried, self-assured presence.

Calm Breathing

Ridiculous as it soundest is possible that in our 50s we never actually learned how to breathe correctly!

Breath is the invisible foundation of poise. Deep, intentional breathing calms the mind, steadies the voice, and enhances presence. A few refined practices:

Breathe through the nose, allowing the breath to expand naturally into the ribs.

Speak at a measured pace—clarity and calmness convey quiet confidence.

In moments of stress, take a pause, inhale deeply, and exhale slowly before responding.

Cheat Sheet

Stand Tall–think elegant thoughts. (Works surprisingly well!) Aim for relaxed, upright posture with no stiffness.
Move with Intention–whether reaching for a glass of water or entering a room, every movement is with ease and purpose
Refine Your daily walk–aim for smooth, natural steps—neither hurried nor overly cautious. Choosing comfortable shoes is a must.
Master the Art of Stillness–sometimes, presence is about knowing when not to fidget or overreact. No drama please!
Dress for the Body You Stand Tall In–clothes should enhance, not restrict, movement. No outfit will look good if you are constantly having to adjust it.
Politeness is Power–a warm smile, a gracious thank you, and a well-placed pause in conversation all convey quiet assurance.

Grace and poise are definitely not about unattainable perfection. It's about moving through the world with a sense of ease, humour and quiet confidence. And that, more than any trend, is what makes a wonderful, long lasting impression.

Luxury at Home: The Wardrobe Beyond Clothes

Dressing beautifully for yourself, even in your most relaxed moments.

True Quiet Luxury is very quiet. It's about getting into small daily luxury habits. Getting up early in the morning and having a few luxurious minutes on your yoga mat, breathing with intention, enjoying a cup of freshly made coffee—followed by paying attention to meticulous dressing, even when there is no where to go.

Allowing ourselves the pleasure of feeling beautiful. Whether it's our yoga session or putting on lipstick, those simple acts make us feel good and in the present moment. Our inner joy is in fact our gift to the world. It's not just about having the perfectly tailored coat or the ideal handbag—it's about how you feel magnificent in your own space, away from the gaze of the world, (or away from social media for that matter).

Dressing beautifully shouldn't stop the moment you close the front door. In fact, the most refined women understand that elegance is more about personal comfort than about public presentation. Less about impressing others and more about indulging in life's small luxuries: the feel of clean pyjamas, the warmth of cashmere socks, the savouring of drinking a choice tea blend from your beautiful porcelain cup rather than a chipped office mug.

Effortless comfort—dressing in a way that feels indulgent yet practical, surrounding yourself with small pleasures that elevate the everyday. Why on earth shuffle around in an old stained sweatshirt when a soft beautiful robe is there waiting for you?

Quiet luxury at home is about the details that make life feel just a little more special, especially in the moments no one else sees. Eating simple fresh food, keeping an eye on healthy weight without deprivation or harsh regimes is a way to show that we care. Exercise should be all about the joy of movement, yoga, meditation, breathing inner calm.

In your 50s and beyond you may live in a small city flat, a rural farm or a large townhouse, but make it your own. This really is a whole subject in itself, but in a nutshell: Time to Surround yourself with uplifting art, furniture you love, colours you adore! (*See resources or check out the 'Old Money Interiors Guide'* ISBN: 978-0-9571233-2-8)

Practical Ways to Bring Luxury into Your Everyday Life

- **The Softest Layers**–a cashmere wrap for chilly mornings, cotton pyjamas that feel like a dream against your skin, and well-made slippers that don't look like they've survived a decade of hard labor.
- **Beautiful Little Rituals**–a coffee cup you actually love, a small silver or lacquer tray for your bedside essentials, and fresh flowers in your kitchen—little things that make the ordinary feel extraordinary.
- **Jewellery Deserves a Proper Home**–a velvet-lined jewellery box, not a tangled heap in the bathroom drawer. Nothing ruins the feeling of quiet luxury faster

than spending half an hour every morning, trying to untangle your beloved understated jewellery.

- **Fresh Sheets, on the bed**–is there a greater luxury than sliding into a bed made with percale cotton or linen sheets? Bonus points if they smell of lavender.
- **Invest in the Unseen**–beautiful lingerie, even if its only you who knows it's there. A well-made robe that feels absolutely delicious. Luxurious hand cream on the nightstand—well cared for hands whisper finesse.

Old Money knows that he essence of quiet luxury at home is to elevate the everyday, take pleasure in the small things. Invest in the power of laundered sheets, fresh flowers and perhaps even a good pair of socks!

Every day is a special event, worth of our dressing well for—showing up as our very best self.

Relationships: the Inner Circle for classic Quiet Luxury Style

Behind every well-dressed woman, there is a trusted network of skilled professionals. These relationships are cultivated over time to ensure that every detail of her appearance is polished to perfection.

It has been said that is not what you know, but WHO you know that matters. Choose your people with care and reward them with appreciation for their skill and respect for their time.

The **tailor** is not just someone who alters clothing; they are your personal stylist. A good tailor is a master of detail, fit and proportion. If you are new to this, start with basic adjustments like hemming your dress, before moving on to more complex tailoring. Best not to haggle, but always agree on the cost beforehand.

The qualified **dermatologist** can help navigating the very expensive, 'anti aging' industry trap. Maintaining healthy, glowing skin is about good hydration, sleep and simple exercise routines.

Regular visits to your talented **hairdresser** are essential —not just for precision cuts, but for maintaining hair health, enhancing colour, and ensuring timeless elegance. Similarly, a **dental hygienist and dentist** keep your smile pristine with regular cleanings and subtle cosmetic enhancements.

Include on your team an experienced **yoga teacher, or personal trainer.** Pick someone that you like and is not too much of a tyrant, but is assertive enough to keep you going. Weekly sessions are invaluable for posture, flexibility, overall calm and well-being. Elegance is not just about clothing but also how we move and carry ourselves. Self discipline and a dedicated practice will increase grace, elegance and finesse as the years go by.

Friendly Boutique owners, vintage specialists, and luxury resale associates who know your taste, can alert you to rare finds. And, of course, Hermès is notorious for requiring an established relationship before offering their most exclusive pieces.
Cultivating these relationships takes time, but the rewards are undeniable, they will make life flow with more ease. Keep interactions warm and cordial—light conversations about travel, family traditions, or art create the perfect balance of familiarity and discretion.

Of course you may no longer shop that much—nowadays you prefer to direct funds to favourite charities and good causes. A legacy is an aristocratic, quiet luxury mindset!

The team for Quiet Luxury with a touch of 'old money' style after 50 (or even before!)

- **Tailor / Seamstress**–for impeccable alterations and custom tailoring.
- **Dermatologist**–for skin health expertise.
- **Hairdresser**–for classic, well-maintained styles. Update your look every few years, it will feel like the elixir of youth!
- **Dental Hygienist & Dentist** – for healthy teeth and subtle cosmetic work.
- **Yoga Teacher**–for posture, flexibility, and overall well-being.
- **Luxury Sales Associate**–for access to exclusive pieces and personal shopping.
- **Vintage & Resale Experts**–for sourcing timeless designer finds.
- **Shoemaker/Cobbler**–for maintaining and restoring luxury footwear.
- **Jeweller**–for care, repair, advice and curation of heirloom pieces.

This style is built on quality, relationships, and discretion—your personal team is there to offer help as and when needed. Thank you team!

What NOT to buy List

Quiet Luxury wardrobe cheat sheet

❌ **Cheap Synthetic Fabrics**: they don't drape well, don't last, your skin can't breathe and they never look expensive. Some of these fabrics should come with a health warning! They are treated with chemicals that can act as endocrine (hormone) disruptors, particularly those used in wrinkle resistance, stain resistance, and so called moisture-wicking properties.

❌ **Polyester**: made from petrochemicals, polyester can release microplastics and is often treated with perfluorinated chemicals (PFCs), which have been linked to endocrine disruption. It can contain antimony, a toxic heavy metal used in production.

❌ **Nylon**: common in activewear, nylon is often treated with phthalates, which can interfere with hormone function. Sweat and heat can increase the absorption of these chemicals into the skin. Avoid at all times, especially during menopause.

❌ **Acrylic**: Contains acrylonitrile, a known carcinogen and potential hormone disruptor. Can release harmful chemicals when heated or washed.

❌ **Rayon (Viscose, Modal, Lyocell, Bamboo Rayon):** though derived from natural sources, the processing involves heavy chemical treatments like carbon disulfide, linked to hormonal imbalances.

Sadly Bamboo rayon, marketed as 'eco-friendly,' often undergoes the same chemical-heavy process. Look for OEKO-TEX® or GOTS certifications to ensure fabric safety.

✖ **Spandex** (Elastane, Lycra): Frequently blended into leggings, and underwear, spandex contains polyurethane, which can release toxic isocyanates known to affect hormones. Just say NO!

How to Reduce Exposure?

It is difficult to avoid these fabrics altogether but at least avoid buying items that come in direct contact with skin.

Choose untreated natural fibres.

Opt for untreated fabrics without wrinkle resistance or stain protection.

Look for OEKO-TEX® or GOTS certifications to ensure fabric safety.

✖ **Overly Trendy Items**: fast fashion buys that even your teenage niece doesn't want.

✖ **Obvious Logos**: anything with huge designer branding screams of status-seeking rather than effortless style.

✖ **Uncomfortable Shoes**: if you cannot happily walk in them for an hour, they are not elegant. We don't ruin our feet!

✖ **Excessively Tight or Ill-Fitting Clothes**: Clothes should skim the body, neither squeeze nor sag.

✖ **Loud, Busy Prints**: Opt for refined neutrals, subtle patterns, or timeless solids instead.

✖ **Overly Ornate Jewellery**: Gaudy, oversized, or heavily branded pieces sometimes look a little desperate.

✖ **Cheap, shapeless or overdecorated Handbags:** – Leather, suede, or structured fabric are far more refined.

✖ **Tacky Accessories:** Neon, overly embellished, or cheaply made? Best not.

Quiet Luxury Life: your 50s & beyond a New Chapter Unfolds

Think of it as evolution rather than aging: A grand opportunity to create a lifestyle marked by elegance, poise, and an appreciation for timeless beauty.

This stage really should not be defined as aging—it's about evolving. A life well-lived refines itself over time, becoming calmer, more assured, a Grande Dame steeped in quiet confidence.

By the time a woman reaches her 50s, she has acquired something more valuable than any designer handbag or bespoke suit—*generosity* and *wisdom*. Quiet Luxury at this stage isn't about accumulating more; it's about *perfecting what is already there.* It is about removing excess, moving through the world with grace, financial discernment, and a wardrobe that reflects ones values.

At this point, a woman's wardrobe nay be well-established, yet refinement remains key. She curates, eliminating what no longer serves her and investing in *better, not more*. Quality tailoring is essential—every piece should *fit impeccably*. Staples like a perfectly structured blazer, a cashmere wrap, and timeless silk blouses become daily uniforms, allowing for elegance without excess.

The Quiet Luxury Lady values discretion over display. She is not chasing trends or over indulging in fleeting luxury. She may invest in *pre-loved Hermès* or commission a hand-finished coat, not because of the label, but because of the craftsmanship. She understands *when* to splurge and *when* to exercise restraint—knowing that understated elegance is the greatest luxury of all.

We move with assurance, we do not *need* to prove anything— presence, choices, and the effortless way we carry ourselves *say it all*. Quiet luxury in one's fifties and beyond is about living well, feeling lovely, and embracing the ease that can only come with time and experience.

This is not an ending; this is a new beginning—one marked by refinement, and elegance.

My wardrobe notes

Get in touch to receive your complimentary **Shopping Resources PDF** – an exclusive, regularly updated list of the finest addresses for Quiet Luxury and Old Money style shopping. please send an email titled: "QL Resources" to henrietta.j.hunter@me.com

henrietta.j.hunter@me.com
https://oldmoneyguides.carrd.co/

Author: Henrietta Jones -Hunter
Publisher: Luminous Publications
Imprint: The 'Gallery
978-0-9571233-8-0

Old Money
Aesthetic
Wardrobe:
fashion & finesse

ISBN:
978-0-9571233-7-3

Old Money
Aesthetic
Interiors:
home living style

ISBN:
978-0-9571233-2-8

Quiet Luxury for
smart money.
fashion style guide:
where to spend &
where to save

ISBN:
978-0-9571233-6-6

Printed in Great Britain
by Amazon

62961926R00060